ULTIMATE STICKER BOOK
MAGICAL ADVENTURES COLLECTION

How to use this book

Read the captions in the 15-page booklet, then turn to the sticker
pages and choose the picture that best fits in the space available.
(Hint: check the sticker labels for clues!)

•

Don't forget that your stickers can be stuck down and peeled off again.

•

There are lots of fantastic extra stickers too!

LONDON, NEW YORK, MUNICH,
MELBOURNE AND DELHI

Edited by Shari Last
Designed by Mark Richards
Jacket designed by Owen Bennett

First published in Great Britain in 2011 by
Dorling Kindersley Limited, 80 Strand, London WC2R 0RL
Penguin Group (UK)

10 9 8 7 6 5 4
008–181147–Jun/11

Page design copyright © 2011 Dorling Kindersley Limited

LEGO, the LEGO logo, the Brick and Knob configurations
and the Minifigure are trademarks of the LEGO Group.
©2011 The LEGO Group.
Produced by Dorling Kindersley Limited under license from the LEGO Group.

A CIP catalogue record for this book is available from the British Library.

ISBN: 978-1-40537-003-5

Colour reproduction by Alta Image, UK
Printed and bound by Graphicom, Italy

Discover more at
www.dk.com
www.LEGO.com
www.warnerbros.com

Harry Potter

Harry Potter thinks he is just an ordinary boy, until he finds out that he is a wizard! In the wizarding world, Harry is known as "The Boy Who Lived".

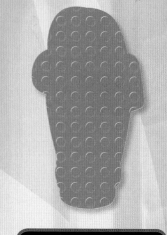

Hedwig
Harry has a pet owl called Hedwig.

Uncle Vernon
Harry's uncle, Vernon Dursley, does not like magic.

Harry Potter
Harry has dark hair, glasses and a lightning-shaped scar on his forehead.

Harry's Wand
Harry's wand has a phoenix feather core.

4 Privet Drive
Harry lives with his uncle, aunt and cousin in a house at 4 Privet Drive.

Student Harry

Harry is in Gryffindor House at Hogwarts.

The Weasleys

The Weasley family lives at The Burrow. Mr and Mrs Weasley have six sons and one daughter.

Scabbers
Ron has a pet rat called Scabbers.

Molly Weasley
Mrs Weasley is Ron's mother and a member of the Order of the Phoenix.

Ginger-Haired Ron Weasley
Ron has ginger hair – like the rest of the Weasley family.

Arthur Weasley
Mr Weasley works for the Ministry of Magic and is interested in Muggle artefacts.

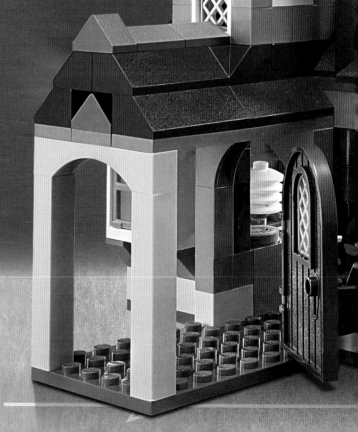

Weasleys' Flying Car
The Weasleys have a flying car.

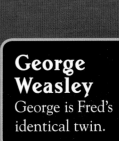

George Weasley
George is Fred's identical twin.

Fred Weasley
Fred is one of Ron's older brothers.

The Burrow

Ginny Weasley
Ron's younger sister is called Ginny.

Wizarding World

The wizarding world is filled with unique creatures, locations and magical items. Harry and his friends are constantly amazed by the wonderful things that they encounter.

Goblin
Gringotts bank is run by Goblins.

Gringotts

GRINGOTTS BANK

Floo Network
Witches and wizards can travel to different locations using the Floo Network.

Wizard Treasure
Gringotts Goblins look after wizard treasure.

Diagon Alley
Diagon Alley is a street full of wizarding shops, including Ollivanders.

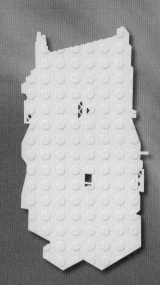

Wizard Pets
Wizards can buy pets in Diagon Alley.

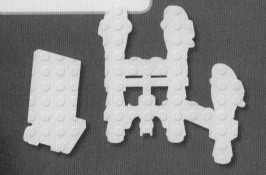

Mr Ollivander
Harry buys his wand from wandmaker, Mr Ollivander.

The Shrieking Shack
The Shrieking Shack is in Hogsmeade.

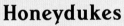

Honeydukes
Honeydukes is a sweet shop in Hogsmeade.

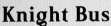

Knight Bus
The Knight Bus is a purple, triple-decker bus that picks up wizards who are stranded.

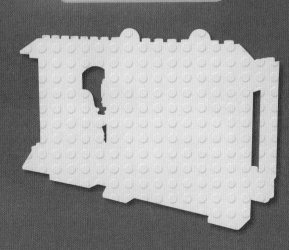

Stan Shunpike
Stan Shunpike is the conductor of the Knight Bus.

Lord Voldemort

Lord Voldemort is known to be the most evil wizard of all time. He and his followers, the Death Eaters, terrorise the wizarding world.

Harry in Year Four
In his fourth year at Hogwarts, Harry battles Lord Voldemort in Little Hangleton graveyard.

Philosopher's Stone
During Harry's first year at Hogwarts, Lord Voldemort tries to obtain the Philosopher's Stone.

Lord Voldemort
Voldemort has white skin and a nose that is flat, like a snake's.

Tom Riddle's Diary
Harry destroys Tom Riddle's diary with a Basilisk fang.

Tom Riddle
Harry meets Tom Riddle in the Chamber of Secrets.

Professor Quirrell
During Harry's first year, Professor Quirrell teaches Defence Against the Dark Arts at Hogwarts, and he possesses a dark secret.

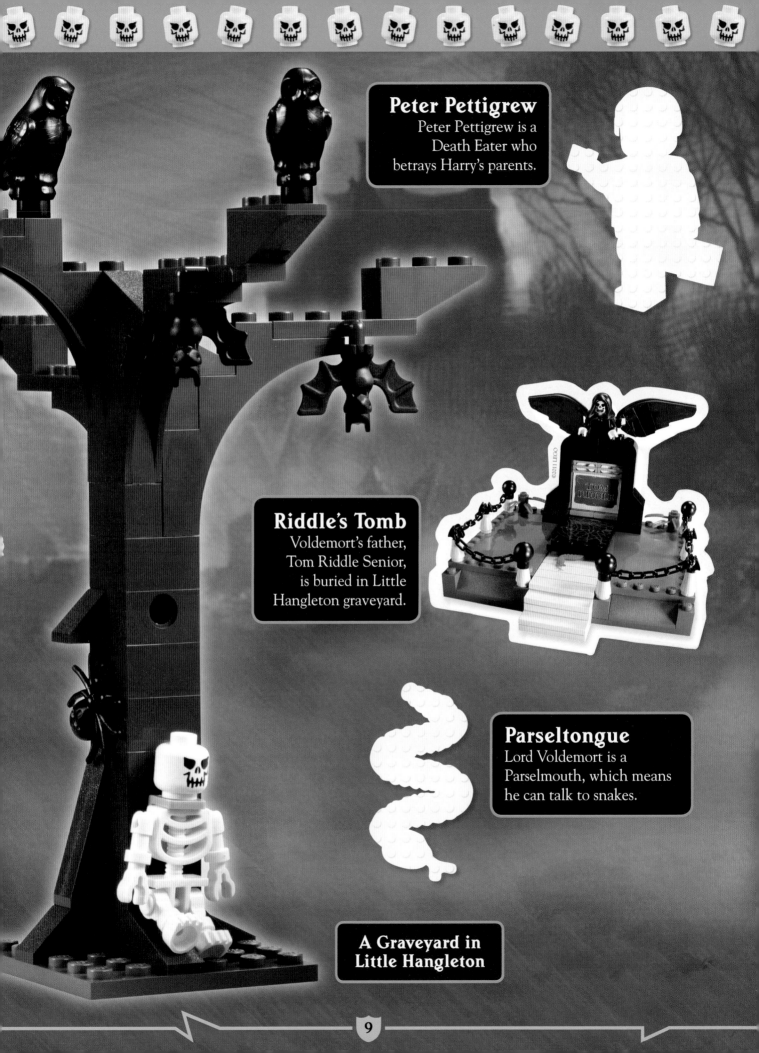

Peter Pettigrew
Peter Pettigrew is a Death Eater who betrays Harry's parents.

Riddle's Tomb
Voldemort's father, Tom Riddle Senior, is buried in Little Hangleton graveyard.

Parseltongue
Lord Voldemort is a Parselmouth, which means he can talk to snakes.

A Graveyard in Little Hangleton

Magical Creatures

The wizarding world is full of extraordinary creatures. Some of these creatures are friendly while others are dangerous.

Dobby
Dobby is a house-elf.

Troll
During Harry's first year, he and Ron defeat a mountain troll in the girls' bathroom.

Boggart
Neville's Boggart takes the form of Professor Snape.

Acromantula

Norwegian Ridgeback
In Harry's first year, Hagrid takes care of a baby dragon called Norbert.

Thestral
Thestrals pull the carriages to Hogwarts.

Hippogriff
In Harry's third year, he and Hermione save a Hippogriff, called Buckbeak, from execution.

Phoenix
Dumbledore has a phoenix called Fawkes.

Fluffy
In Harry's first year, Fluffy guards the Forbidden Corridor in Hogwarts.

Werewolf
Professor Lupin is a werewolf.

Acromantula
Aragog is an Acromantula – a very large spider.

Basilisk
During Harry's second year, he battles a Basilisk in the Chamber of Secrets.

Dark Arts

Lord Voldemort practises the Dark Arts. He uses the Dark Mark to summon his Death Eaters.

He Who Must Not Be Named
Many wizards fear Lord Voldemort and will not utter his name.

Death Eater
Lord Voldemort's followers wear masks and robes.

Werewolf Fenrir Greyback
Fenrir Greyback appears wolf-like, even when the moon is not full.

BORGIN
AND
BURKES

Borgin and Burkes

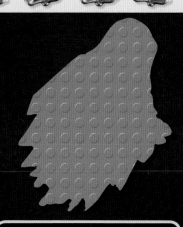

Lucius Malfoy
Draco's father is a Death Eater.

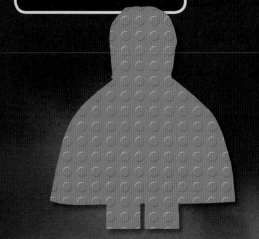

Death Eater Draco Malfoy
In Harry's sixth year, Draco Malfoy becomes a Death Eater.

Dementor's Kiss
Dementors make people feel sadness and despair.

Severus Snape
Severus Snape performs the Unbreakable Vow with Narcissa Malfoy.

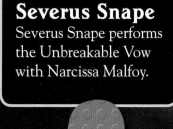

Vincent Crabbe
Crabbe is one of Draco Malfoy's cronies.

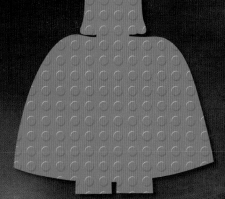

Gregory Goyle
Goyle is another of Draco's Slytherin cronies.

Bellatrix Lestrange
Bellatrix is a loyal Death Eater.

Peter "Wormtail" Pettigrew
Peter Pettigrew is also known as Wormtail.

Fighting Against Evil

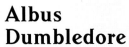

Harry and his friends form Dumbledore's Army in Harry's fifth year. They meet in the Room of Requirement to practise defensive spells.

Albus Dumbledore

Students at Hogwarts name Dumbledore's Army after their Headmaster.

Hermione

Hermione practises spells with Dumbledore's Army.

Fred and George

Fred and George Weasley are proud members of Dumbledore's Army.

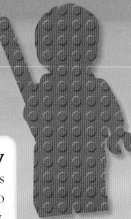

Harry

Harry teaches defensive magic to Dumbledore's Army.

Luna

During Dumbledore's Army meetings, Luna learns to cast the Patronus Charm.

Ginny

Ginny Weasley joins her brothers and friends as part of Dumbledore's Army.

Ron

Ron is proud to
fight as part of
Dumbledore's Army.

Neville

Neville finds the Room
of Requirement where
Dumbledore's Army meets.

**Hogwarts
Castle**

Battle at The Burrow

Bellatrix and Fenrir attack The Burrow. The Weasleys and Harry battle bravely to save the Weasleys' home.

Bellatrix Lestrange at The Burrow

Bellatrix Lestrange taunts Harry as she and Fenrir Greyback attack The Burrow.

Death Eater Fenrir Greyback

Fenrir Greyback attacks The Burrow with Bellatrix Lestrange.

Mrs Weasley

Mrs Weasley defends her family and home from Death Eaters.

Mr Weasley

Mr Weasley joins Harry and Ginny in a battle against Bellatrix and Fenrir at The Burrow.

Harry Reacts

Harry Potter races after Bellatrix when she and fellow Death Eaters attack The Burrow.

Brave Ginny

Ginny follows Harry through the reeds as fire surrounds The Burrow.